A·B·C
Hidden Pictures
Sticker Learning Fun

For information about permission to reproduce selections from this book for
an entire school or school district, please contact permissions@highlights.com.

Published by Highlights Learning • 815 Church Street • Honesdale, Pennsylvania 18431
ISBN: 978-1-64472-184-1
Printed in Shenzhen, Guangdong, China
Mfg. 08/2020 First edition
10 9 8 7 6 5 4 3 2

For assistance in the preparation of this book, the editors would like to thank:
Vanessa Maldonado, MSEd; MS Literacy Ed. K–12; Reading/LA Consultant Cert.; K–5 Literacy Instructional Coach
Jump Start Press, Inc.

A

This is an uppercase A.

a

This is a lowercase a.

Trace the letters. Then write your own.

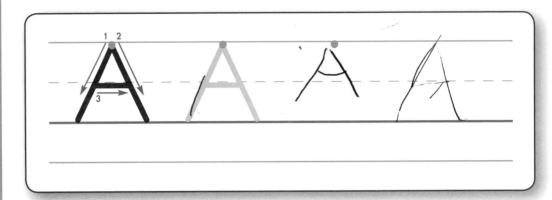

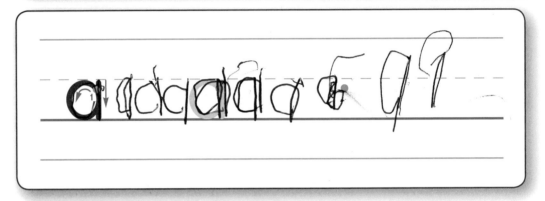

A is for Apple. Circle each A you see in the picture.

Ape Acrobats

This awesome acrobat scene has **8** hidden objects that start with the letter **A**: **Acorn**, **Airplane**, **Alligator**, **Ant**, **Apple**, **Arrow**, **Artist's brush**, and **Ax**. Place a sticker on each one you find.

B

This is an
uppercase B.

b

This is a
lowercase b.

Trace the letters. Then write your own.

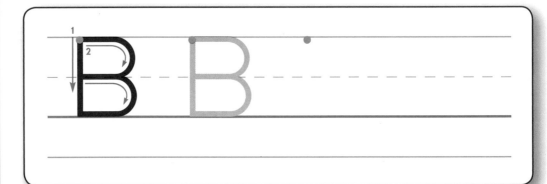

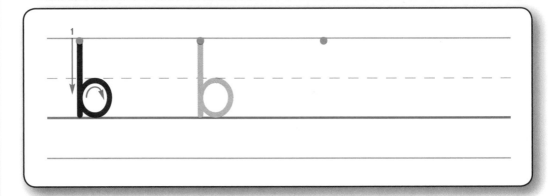

B is for Butterfly. Each beautiful butterfly has one that looks just like it. Draw lines to match the pairs.

Balloon Bee

This balloon-animal scene has **8** hidden objects that start with the letter **B**: **Banana**, **Bell**, **Belt**, **Book**, **Boot**, **Bread**, **Broccoli**, and **Button**. Place a sticker on each one you find.

C

This is an
uppercase C.

c

This is a
lowercase c.

Trace the letters. Then write your own.

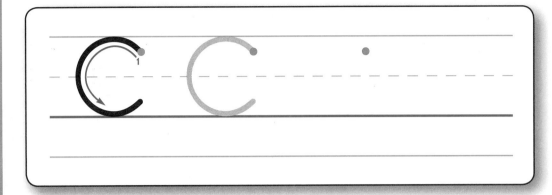

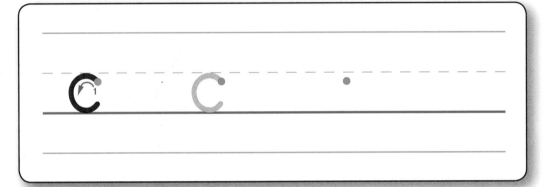

C is for Camel. Circle each C you see in the picture.

Can You Canoe?

This calm canoe scene has 8 hidden objects that start with the letter C: Cake, Can, Coin, Candle, Cane, Comb, Crayon, and Cupcake. Place a sticker on each one you find.

D

This is an uppercase D.

d

This is a lowercase d.

Trace the letters. Then write your own.

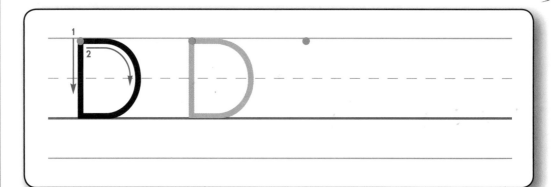

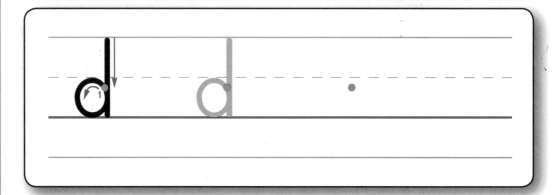

D is for Dinosaur. Color in each shape that has a D with a green crayon. Color in each shape that has a d with a **brown** crayon.

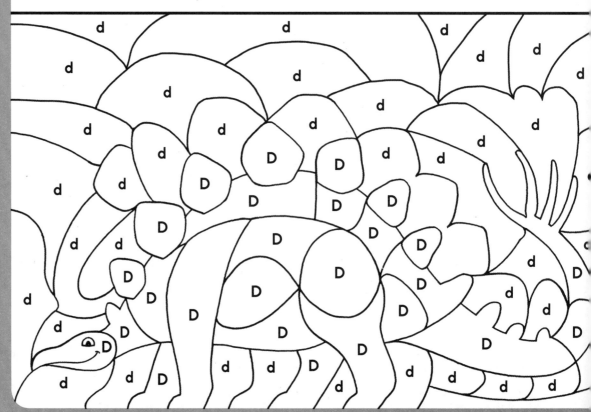

Dragon Dodgeball

This dynamic dodgeball scene has **8** hidden objects that start with the letter **D**: **Dart, Diamond, Dice, Dish, Domino, Doughnut, Drum,** and **Drumstick**. Place a sticker on each one you find.

E

This is an uppercase **E**.

e

This is a lowercase **e**.

Trace the letters. Then write your own.

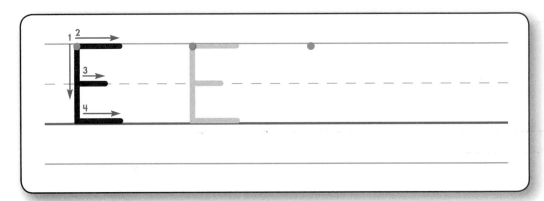

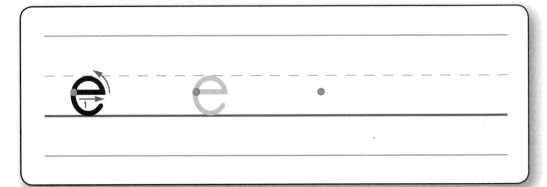

E is for Eagle. Help this eagle find a path to her eggs.

START

FINISH

Elephant Fun

This earring-shopping scene has **8** hidden objects that start with the letter E: **Earmuffs**, **Eel**, **Eggplant**, **Eggshell**, **Egg timer**, **Envelope**, **Eyedropper**, and **Eyeglasses**. Place a sticker on each one you find.

STICKER PUZZLE

F

This is an uppercase F.

f

This is a lowercase f.

Trace the letters. Then write your own.

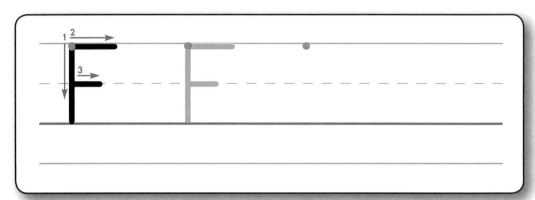

F is for Fish. Each funny fish has one that looks just like it. Draw lines to match the pairs.

Farm Find

This fun farm scene has **8** hidden objects that start with the letter **F**: **Fish, Fishhook, Flag, Flashlight, Flower, Fly, Football,** and **Fork.** Place a sticker on each one you find.

G

This is an uppercase G.

g

This is a lowercase g.

Trace the letters. Then write your own.

G is for Golf. Circle each G you see in the picture.

Page 17

heart

horn

hoe

hammer

horseshoe

hot dog

hat

hanger

Page 19

ice cube

ice-cream cone

iron

ice pop

ice skate

inchworm

igloo

icicle

Page 21

jeep

jellyfish

jelly bean

jet airplane

jug

jack-o'-lantern

jump rope

jar

Page 23

kazoo

kangaroo

koala

ketchup

key

kayak

kite

Page 25

ladle

light bulb

lemon

lollipop

lamp

ladder

lightning bolt

lock

ighlights Highlights Highlights Highlights

Highlights Highlights Highlights Highlight
ighlights Highlights Highlights Highlights
Highlights Highlights Highlights Highlight
ighlights Highlights Highlights Highlights
Highlights Highlights Highlights Highlight
ighlights Highlights Highlights Highlights
Highlights Highlights Highlights Highlight
ighlights Highlights Highlights Highlights

Game Night

This grandparent game scene has **8** hidden objects that start with the letter G: **Gate**, **Ghost**, **Glasses**, **Globe**, **Glove**, **Golf club**, **Grapes**, and **Guitar**. Place a sticker on each one you find.

H

This is an uppercase H.

h

This is a lowercase h.

Trace the letters. Then write your own.

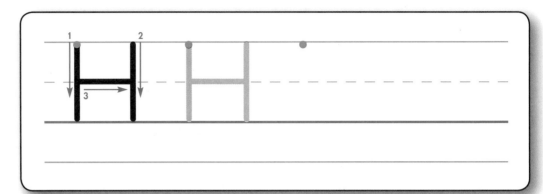

H is for Hat. Follow the paths to see which hat each hedgehog will wear.

Hamster Home

This happy hamster scene has **8** hidden objects that start with the letter **H**: **Hammer**, **Hanger**, **Hat**, **Heart**, **Hoe**, **Hot dog**, **Horn**, and **Horseshoe**. Place a sticker on each one you find.

I

This is an uppercase I.

i

This is a lowercase i.

Trace the letters. Then write your own.

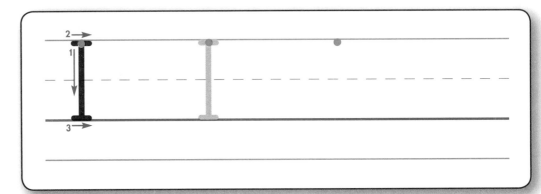

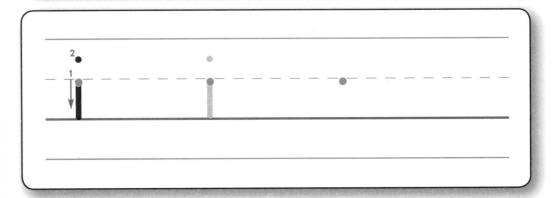

I is for **Ice Cream**. Circle each **I** you see in the picture.

Iguana Island

This island scene has **8** hidden objects that start with the letter I: **Ice-cream cone, Ice cube, Ice pop, Ice skate, Icicle, Igloo, Inchworm,** and **Iron.** Place a sticker on each one you find.

J

This is an uppercase J.

j

This is a lowercase j.

Trace the letters. Then write your own.

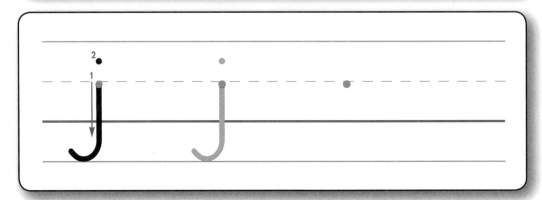

J is for Jack-o'-lantern. Draw a face on this pumpkin to turn it into a jack-o'-lantern!

Just Juggling

This juggling scene has **8** hidden objects that start with the letter **J**: **Jack-o'-lantern**, **Jar**, **Jeep**, **Jelly bean**, **Jellyfish**, **Jet airplane**, **Jug**, and **Jump rope**. Place a sticker on each one you find.

STICKER PUZZLE

K

This is an uppercase K.

k

This is a lowercase k.

Trace the letters. Then write your own.

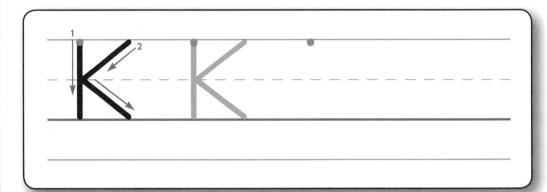

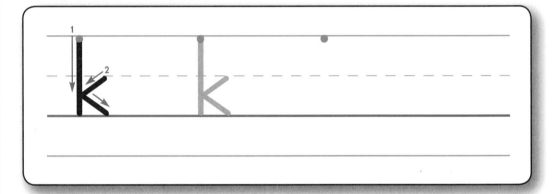

K is for Karate. Circle each K you see in the picture.

Kid Karaoke

STICKER PUZZLE

This karaoke scene has **7** hidden objects that start with the letter K: **Kangaroo, Kayak, Kazoo, Ketchup, Key, Kite,** and **Koala**. Place a sticker on each one you find.

L

This is an uppercase **L**.

l

This is a lowercase **l**.

Trace the letters. Then write your own.

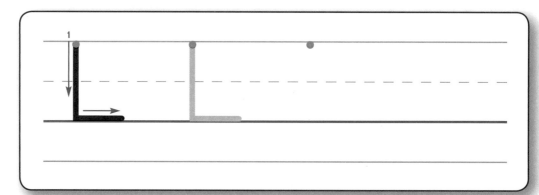

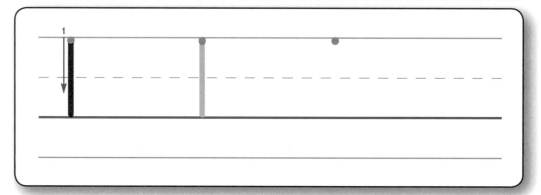

L is for Leaf. Each lovely leaf has one that looks just like it. Draw lines to match the pairs.

Light the Night

This lightning-bug scene has **8** hidden objects that start with the letter L: **Ladder**, **Ladle**, **Lamp**, **Lemon**, **Light bulb**, **Lightning bolt**, **Lock**, and **Lollipop**. Place a sticker on each one you find.

STICKER PUZZLE

M

This is an
uppercase M.

This is a
lowercase m.

Trace the letters. Then write your own.

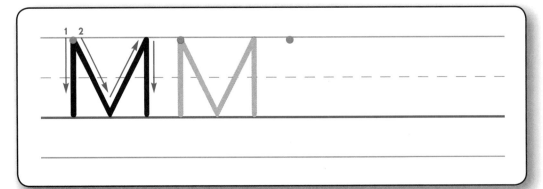

M is for Mutts. Each cute mutt has one that looks just like it.
Draw lines to match the pairs.

Music Makers

This merry music scene has **8** hidden objects that start with the letter M: **Magnifying glass, Microphone, Mitten, Moon, Mop, Muffin, Mug,** and **Mushroom.** Place a sticker on each one you find.

N

n

This is an
uppercase **N**.

This is a
lowercase **n**.

Trace the letters. Then write your own.

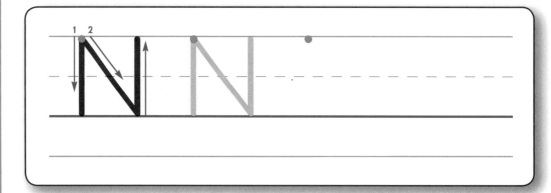

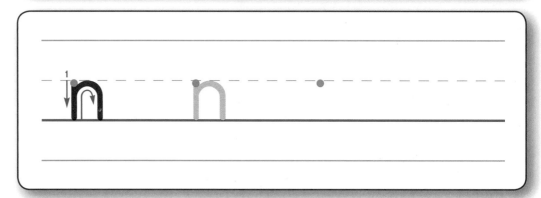

N is for Newt. Color in each shape that has an **N** with an **orange** crayon .
Color in each shape that has an **n** with a **green** crayon.

New Neighbors

This neighborhood scene has **8** hidden objects that start with the letter N: **Nail**, **Necklace**, **Necktie**, **Needle**, **Newt**, **Nickel**, **Noodle**, and **Notebook**. Place a sticker on each one you find.

This is an uppercase O.

This is a lowercase o.

Trace the letters. Then write your own.

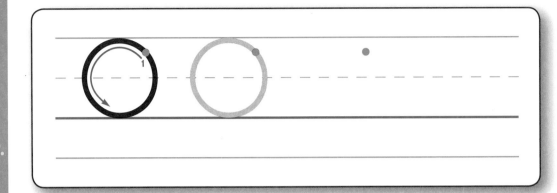

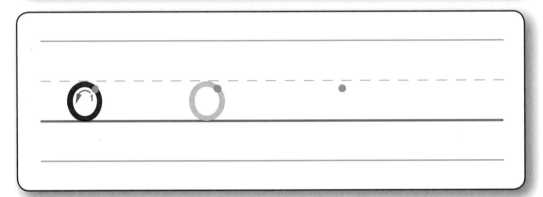

O is for Owl. Draw an X to cross out the owl in each row that does not match the others.

Owl Origami

This origami-making scene has **8** hidden objects that start with the letter O: **Oar**, **Octagon**, **Octopus**, **Olive**, **Onion**, **Orange**, **Ornament**, and **Oven mitt**. Place a sticker on each one you find.

STICKER PUZZLE

P

This is an uppercase **P**.

p

This is a lowercase **p**.

Trace the letters. Then write your own.

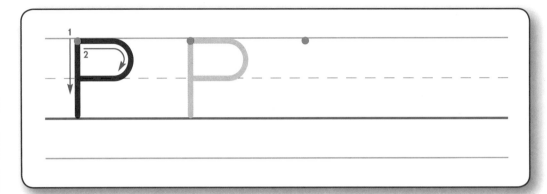

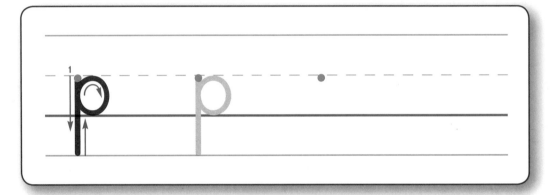

P is for Piano. Draw a line between the **2** pianos that look the same.

Pig Pajama Party

This pajama party has **8** hidden objects that start with the letter **P**: **Paintbrush**, **Pants**, **Peanut**, **Peapod**, **Pear**, **Pen**, **Pickle**, and **Popcorn**. Place a sticker on each one you find.

STICKER PUZZLE

Q

This is an
uppercase Q.

q

This is a
lowercase q.

Trace the letters. Then write your own.

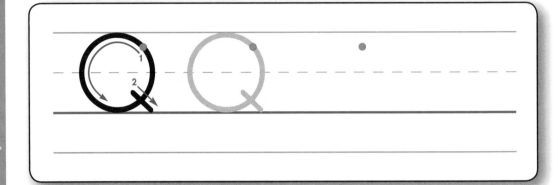

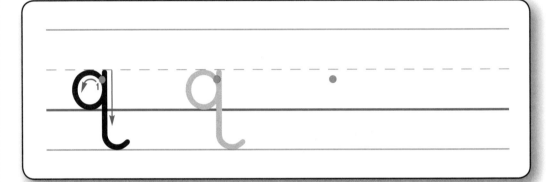

Q is for Quail. Place one of your stickers
next to each quail to make 4 matching pairs.

STICKER PUZZLE

Quilting Queen

Trace the letter Q. Then draw a design on the queen's new quilt.

R

This is an
uppercase R.

r

This is a
lowercase r.

Trace the letters. Then write your own.

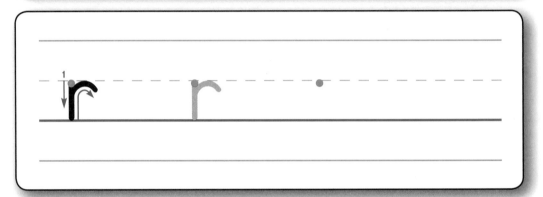

R is for Rooster. Follow the path to help this
rooster meet his friend.

FINISH

START

Raft Ride

This rapid raft ride has **8** hidden objects that start with the letter R: **Racket**, **Rake**, **Ring**, **Rocket ship**, **Rolling pin**, **Rope**, **Rose**, and **Ruler**. Place a sticker on each one you find.

STICKER PUZZLE

S

This is an uppercase S.

s

This is a lowercase s.

Trace the letters. Then write your own.

S is for Snowman. Draw a smile on this silly snowman. What other things do you see that start with the S sound?

Swing Set

This swing-set scene has **8** hidden objects that start with the letter **S**: **Safety pin**, **Sailboat**, **Saw**, **Screwdriver**, **Seashell**, **Snake**, **Spoon**, and **Suitcase**. Place a sticker on each one you find.

T

This is an uppercase T.

This is a lowercase t.

Trace the letters. Then write your own.

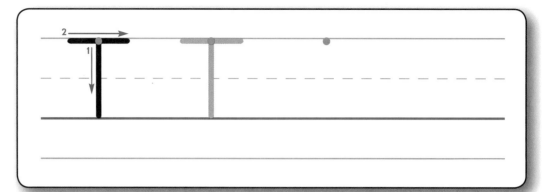

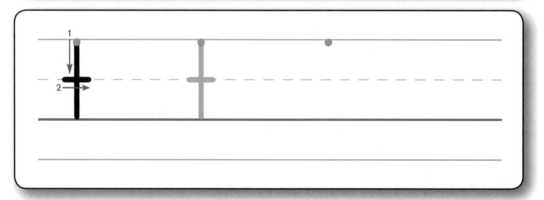

T is for Turkey. Circle each T you see in the picture.

Tea, Rex?

This tea shop scene has **8** hidden objects that start with the letter T: **Telescope**, **Tennis ball**, **Tent**, **Tomato**, **Toothbrush**, **Toothpaste**, **Trowel**, and **Tweezers**. Place a sticker on each one you find.

STICKER PUZZLE

U

This is an
uppercase U.

u

This is a
lowercase u.

Trace the letters. Then write your own.

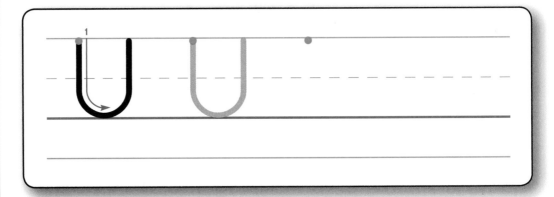

U is for Unicycle. Circle the differences you see between these 2 pictures.

Unicycling Unicorn

Place your unicorn sticker at **START**. Then follow the U's to help the unicorn get to the umbrella shop.

V

This is an uppercase V.

v

This is a lowercase v.

Trace the letters. Then write your own.

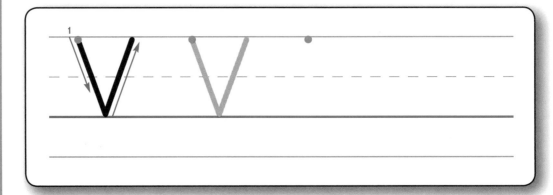

V is for Vegetable. Draw an ✕ to cross out the vegetable in each row that does not match the others.

Volleyball Victory

This volleyball game has **8** hidden objects that start with the letter V: **Vacuum**, **Valentine**, **Van**, **Vase**, **Vest**, **Vine**, **Violin**, and **Volcano**. Place a sticker on each one you find.

STICKER PUZZLE

19:35

Vultures 21

Voles 24

This is an
uppercase W.

This is a
lowercase w.

Trace the letters. Then write your own.

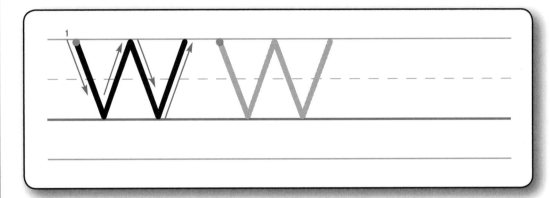

W is for Watermelon. Each slice of watermelon has one that looks just like it. Draw lines to match the pairs.

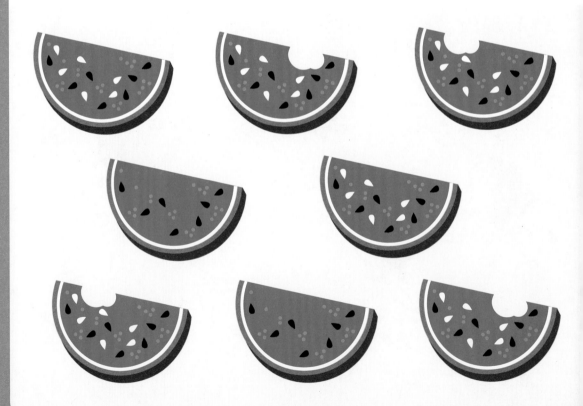

Witch Way?

This wacky witch scene has **8** hidden objects that start with the letter W: **Waffle, Watering can, Whale, Whistle, Worm, Wok, Wrench,** and **Wristwatch.** Place a sticker on each one you find.

STICKER PUZZLE

GHOSTERY STORE

DAYSCARE CENTER

WANDERFUL WAFFLES

GHOST OFFICE

BROOM PERFUME

SANDWITCH SHOP

This is an uppercase **X**.

This is a lowercase **x**.

Trace the letters. Then write your own.

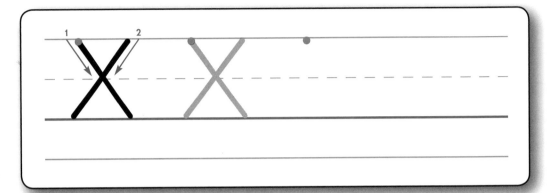

X is in Fox. Circle each **X** you see in this picture of Xavier Fox and his mom.

Taxi Time

Place your Fox family sticker at START. Then help the Foxes find a path to their taxi.

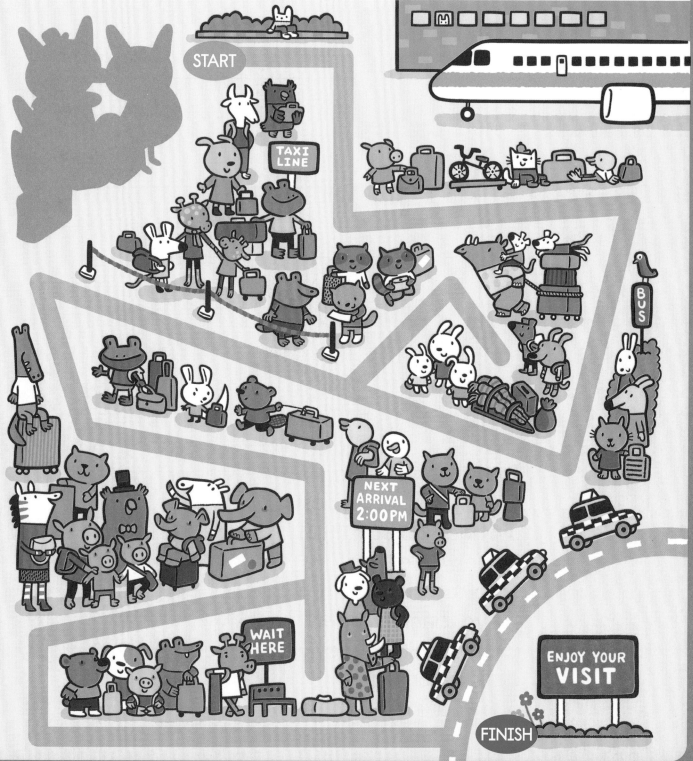

Y

This is an uppercase Y.

y

This is a lowercase y.

Trace the letters. Then write your own.

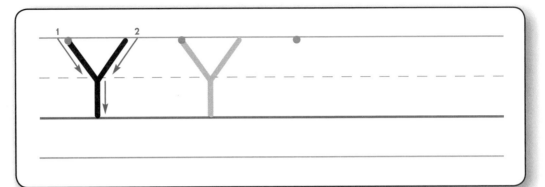

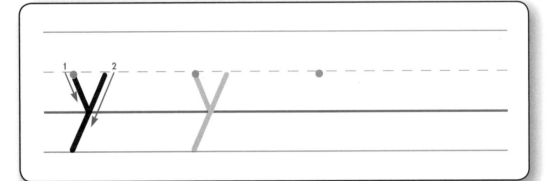

Yak and Zebras

This yak and zebra tug-of-war scene has **6** hidden objects that begin with either **Y** or **Z**: **Yardstick, Yarn, Yo-yo, Zinnia, Zipper,** and **Zucchini**. Place a sticker on each one you find.

Z

This is an uppercase Z.

z

This is a lowercase y.

Trace the letters. Then write your own.

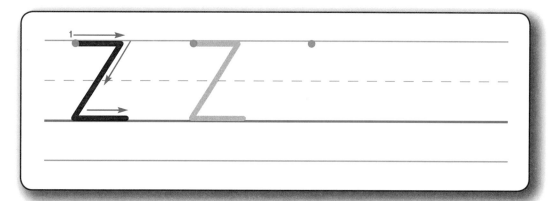

STICKER PUZZLE

Letter Match

STICKER PUZZLE

Place each sticker next to the correct letter. Then draw lines to match each uppercase letter to its lowercase letter.

 A ○   ○ e

 B ○   ○ d

 C ○   ○ c

 D ○   ○ b

 E ○   ○ f

 F ○   ○ a

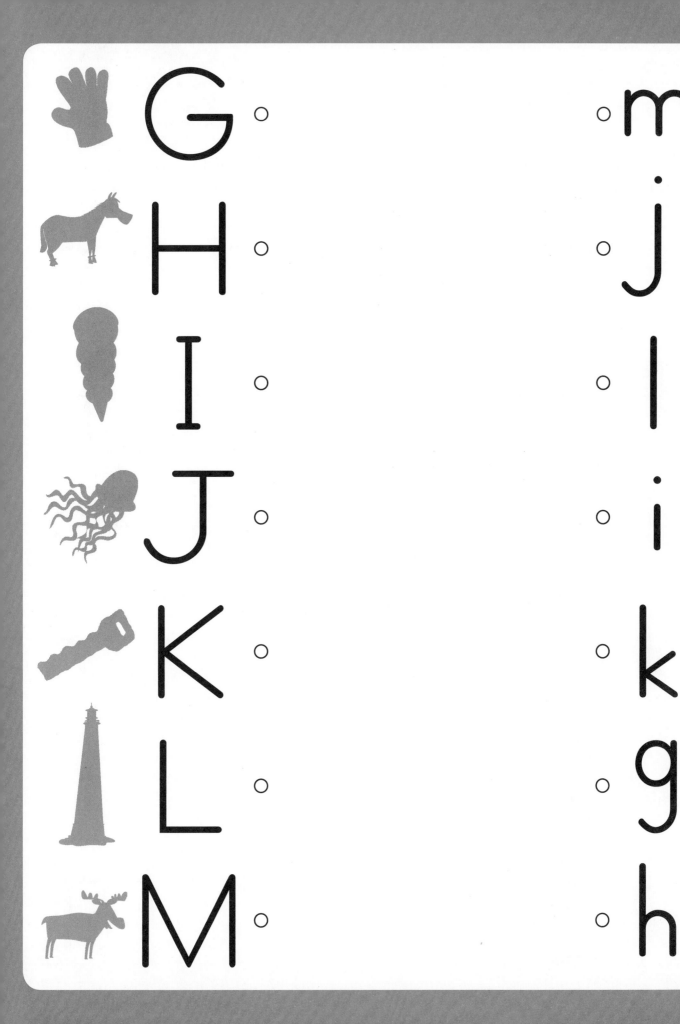

G   ◦   ◦ m

H   ◦   ◦ j

I   ◦   ◦ l

J   ◦   ◦ i

K   ◦   ◦ k

L   ◦   ◦ g

M   ◦   ◦ h

Letter Match

Place each sticker next to the correct letter. Then draw lines to match each uppercase letter to its lowercase letter.

 N ○   ○ o

 O ○   ○ p

 P ○   ○ s

 Q ○   ○ r

 R ○   ○ n

S ○   ○ q

T   ○

U   ○

V   ○

W   ○

X   ○

Y   ○

Z   ○

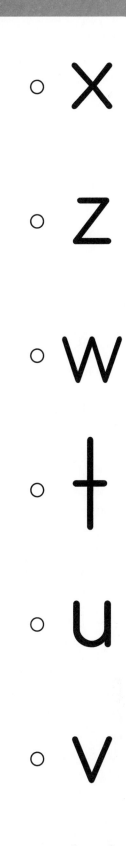

○   x

○   z

○   w

○   t

○   u

○   v

○   y

ABC Order

Place your uppercase stickers in the correct spots to complete the alphabet and help Andy reach Planet Zeetz.

abc Order

Place your lowercase stickers in the correct spots to complete the alphabet and help Alli reach her friend Zippy.

A to Z

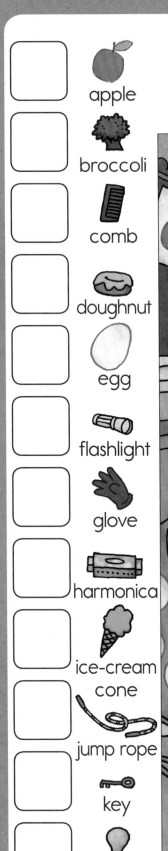

- apple
- broccoli
- comb
- doughnut
- egg
- flashlight
- glove
- harmonica
- ice-cream cone
- jump rope
- key
- light bulb
- mitten

This classroom has **26** hidden objects—one for each letter of the alphabet! Circle each one you find. Place each letter sticker next to the correct object.

nail

olive

paper clip

question mark

ruler

sock

toothbrush

umbrella

vase

wristwatch

xylophone

yo-yo

zipper

Answers

Page 2
Aa

Page 3
Ape Acrobats

Page 4
Bb
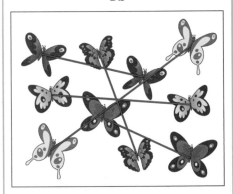

Page 5
Balloon Bee

Page 6
Cc

Page 7
Can You Canoe?

Page 9
Dragon Dodgeball

Page 10
Ee
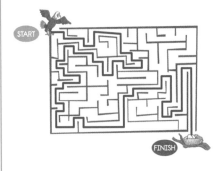

Page 11
Elephant Fun

Answers

Page 12
Ff

Page 13
Farm Find

Page 14
Gg

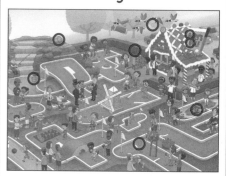

Page 15
Game Night

Page 16
Hh

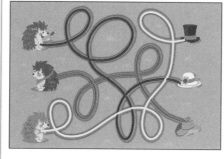

Page 17
Hamster Home

Page 18
Ii

Page 19
Iguana Island

Page 21
Just Juggling

Answers

Page 22
Kk

Page 23
Kid Karaoke

Page 24
Ll

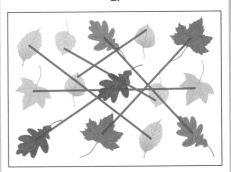

Page 25
Light the Night

Page 26
Mm

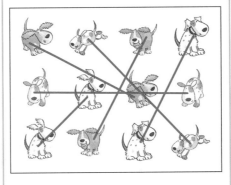

Page 27
Music Makers

Page 29
New Neighbors

Page 30
Oo

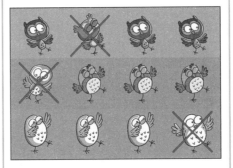

Page 31
Owl Origami

Answers

Page 32
Pp

Page 33
Pig Pajama Party

Page 36
Rr

Page 37
Raft Ride

Page 39
Swing Set

Page 40
Tt

Page 41
Tea, Rex?

Page 42
Uu

Page 43
Unicycling Unicorn

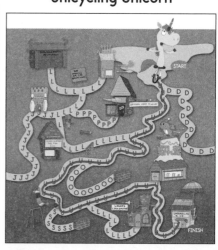

Answers

Page 44
Vv
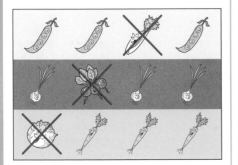

Page 45
Volleyball Victory

Page 46
Ww
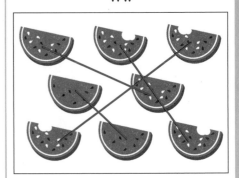

Page 47
Witch Way?

Page 48
Xx

Page 49
Taxi Time

Page 51
Yak and Zebras

Page 52
Letter Match
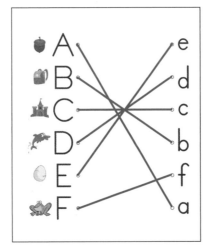

Page 53
Letter Match

Page 27

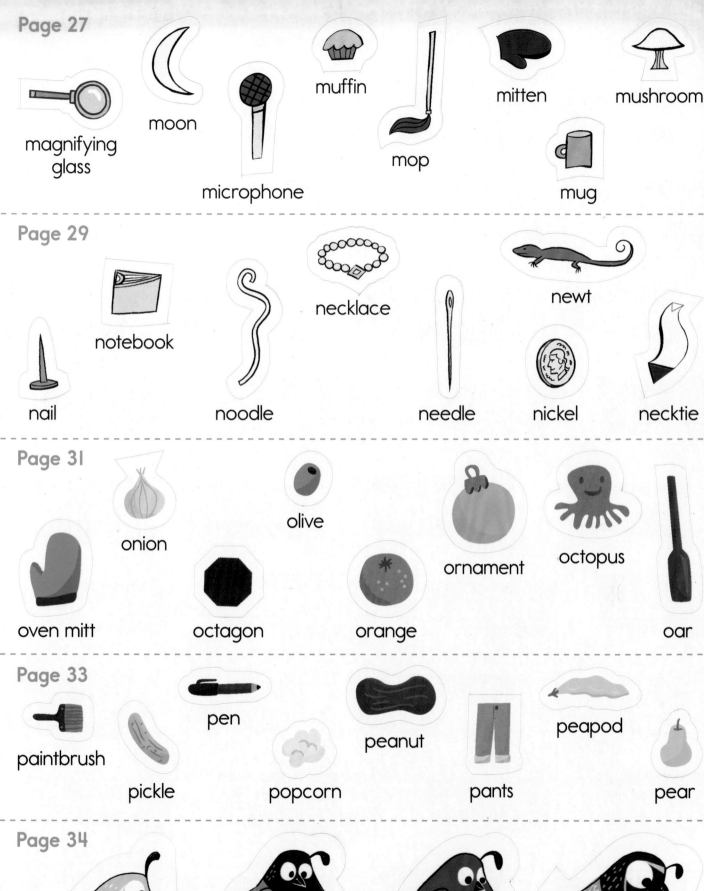

magnifying glass

moon

microphone

muffin

mop

mitten

mushroom

mug

Page 29

notebook

necklace

newt

nail

noodle

needle

nickel

necktie

Page 31

onion

olive

ornament

octopus

oven mitt

octagon

orange

oar

Page 33

paintbrush

pickle

pen

peanut

peapod

popcorn

pants

pear

Page 34

Highlights

Page 37

rake

racket

ruler

rolling pin

rope

rocket ship

rose

ring

Page 39

spoon

saw

suitcase

seashell

safety pin

sailboat

snake

screwdriver

Page 41

tennis ball

toothbrush

toothpaste

trowel

tweezers

tent

telescope

tomato

Page 43

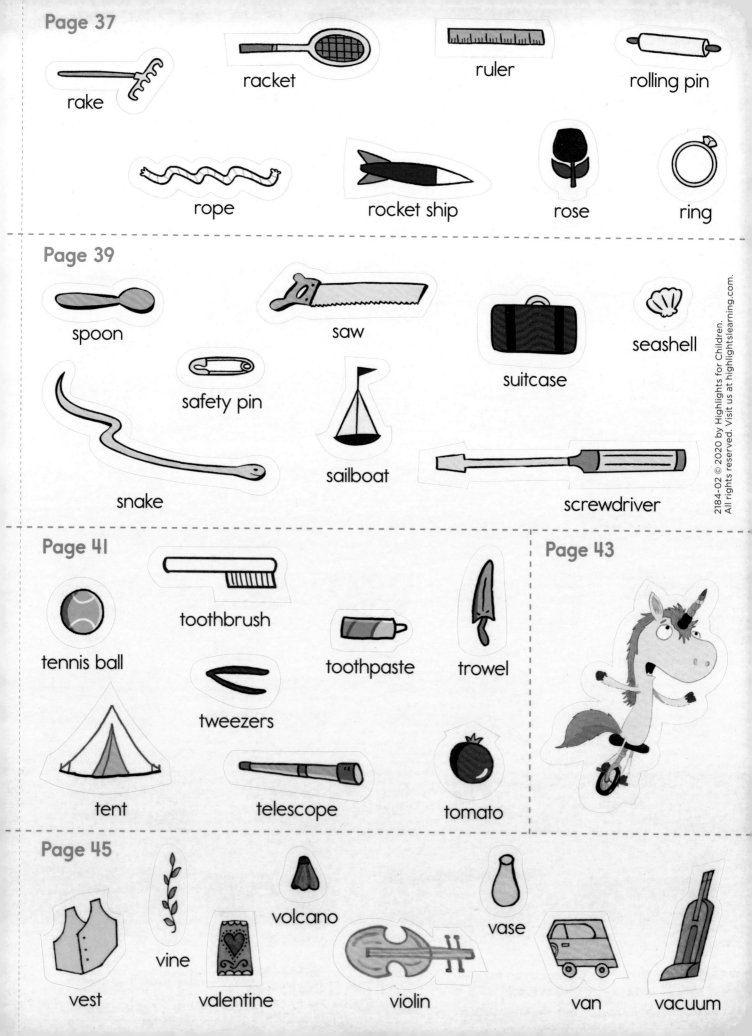

Page 45

vest

vine

volcano

valentine

violin

vase

van

vacuum

watering
can

wristwatch

wok

waffle

whistle

worm

wrench

whale

zipper

yardstick

zinnia

zucchini

yarn

yo-yo

E N U Y S

Q K W I B

r w v t o g

h j l d c

acorn

backpack

castle

dolphin

egg

frog

glove

horse

ice-cream cone

jellyfish

key

lighthouse

moose

pig

nest

quilt

orange

ruler

scissors

tractor

umbrella

volcano

yo-yo

X-ray

zipper

whale

Pages 58–59

A B C D E F G H I
J K L M N O P Q R
S T U V W X Y Z

Bonus stickers! Use these to mark your favorite puzzles, or share them with friends.